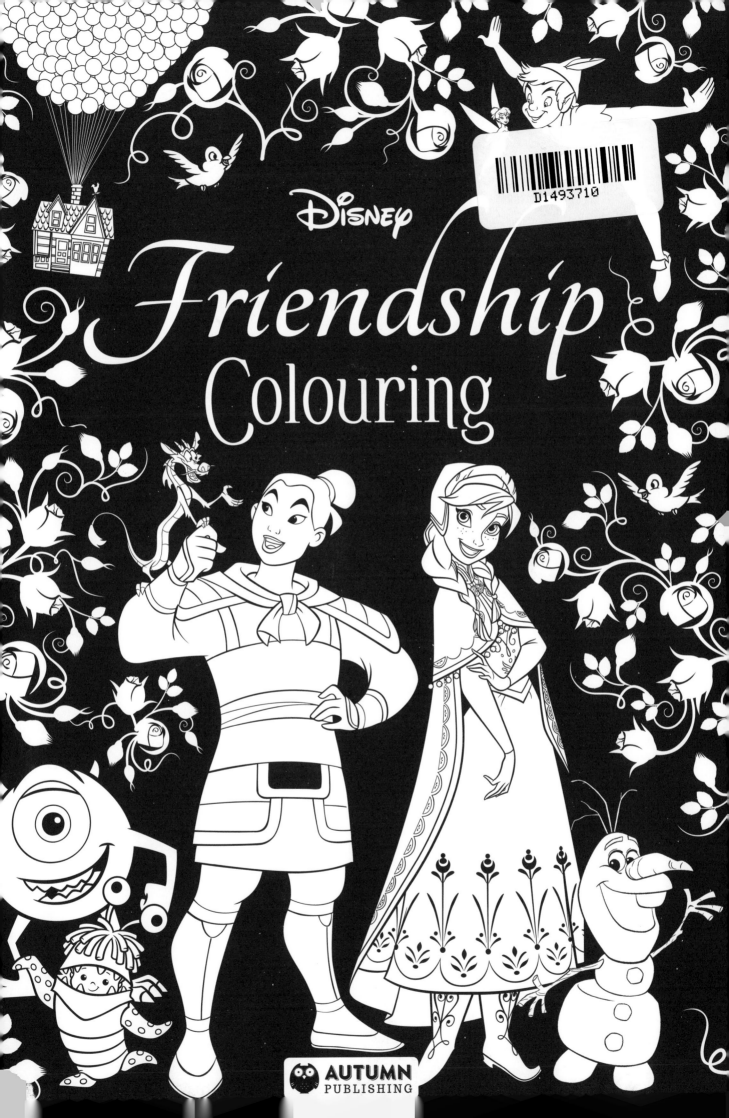

Disney

Friendship
Colouring

AUTUMN
PUBLISHING

AUTUMN
PUBLISHING

Published in 2022
First published in the UK by Autumn Publishing
An imprint of Igloo Books Ltd
Cottage Farm, NN6 0BJ, UK
Owned by Bonnier Books
Sveavägen 56, Stockholm, Sweden
www.igloobooks.com

0622 006
6 8 10 12 13 11 9 7
ISBN 978-1-83903-128-1

Printed and manufactured in China

The Magic of Friendship

Friendships come in all shapes and sizes. Some friendships are new, some we've had all our lives. You may have met your best friend on your first day of school, or in a random twist of fate. But no matter the foundations of a relationship, friends enrich, inspire and support us throughout our lives.

This colouring book celebrates the joy of friendship, and honours some of Disney's most heart-warming duos who draw on each other's strengths to overcome any hurdles they endure. From Peter Pan and Tinker Bell battling the villainous Captain Hook together, to Dumbo and Timothy Mouse believing in each other when no one else did, these inspirational friendships have made us laugh and made us cry for over 80 years.

Filled with gorgeous artwork, this book brings the magic of love and friendship to life, as you colour these wonderful characters who share a bond like no other.

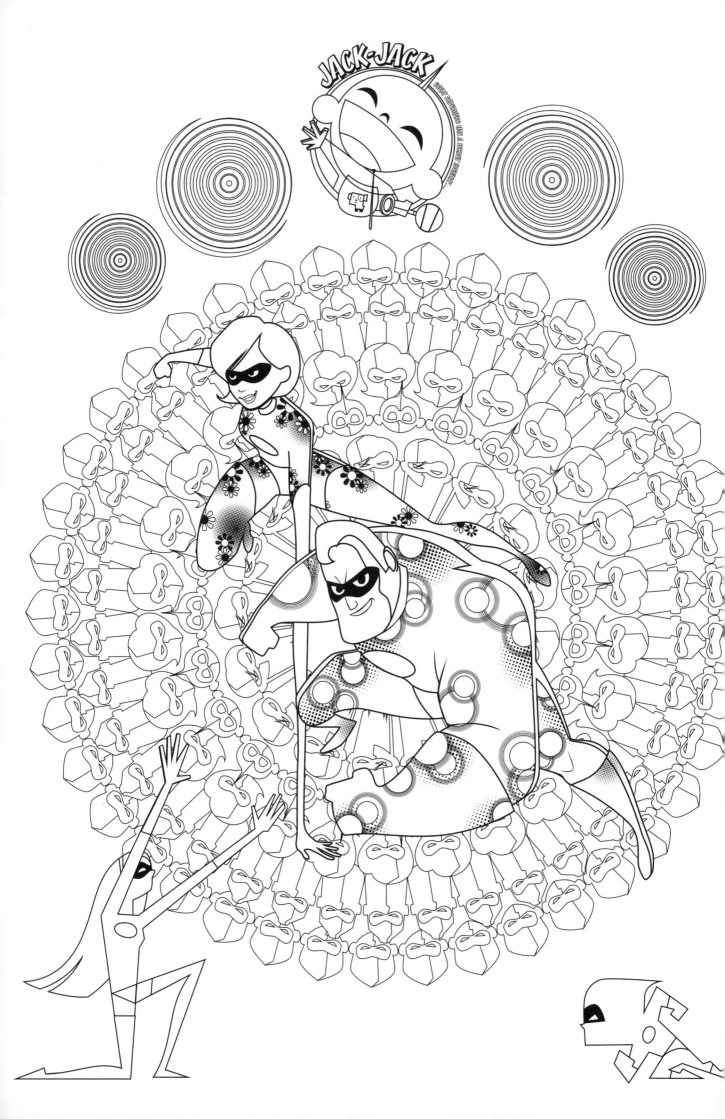

MAKE YOUR MARK
ARLO and SPOT

THANKS FOR
STAYING WITH ME

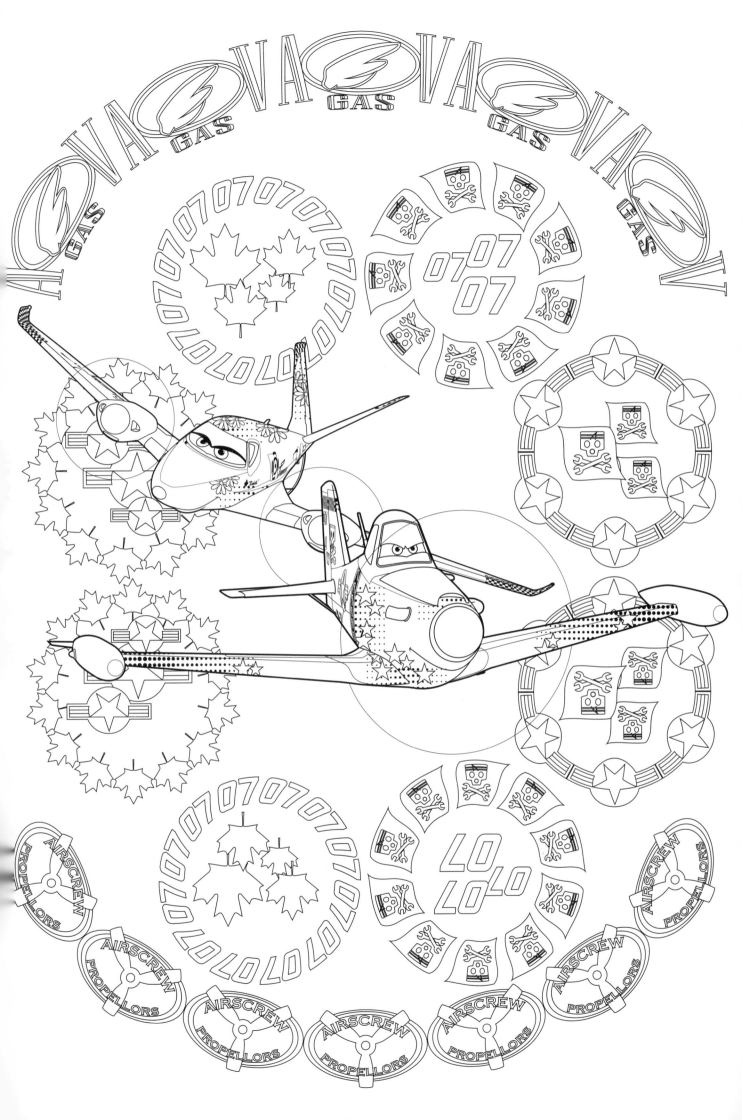